CORNISH LEGENDS

Robert Hunt

Sept/04

To Charlie
with love from
Granny

Tor Mark Press • Redruth

THE TOR MARK SERIES

Published by Tor Mark, PO Box 4, Redruth, Cornwall TR16 5YX
This edition published 1997
Reprinted 2003
© 1997 Tor Mark
ISBN 0-85025-362-4
Cover illustration by Linda Garland

Printed in Great Britain by R Booth (Troutbeck Press), Mabe, Cornwall

Introduction

The stories collected here are taken from Robert Hunt's *Popular Romances of the West of England*, published in 1865.

Hunt was the posthumous son of a naval captain and was born in 1807 at Devonport, then called Plymouth Dock. He went to school in Plymouth and Penzance, then was apprenticed to a surgeon in London. He practised as a physician for five years; while in his early twenties suffered a serious breakdown and resolved to convalesce in the West Country and 'to visit each relic of Old Cornwall and to gather up every existing tale of its ancient people'.

As a child he had visited Bodmin with his mother and heard tales of Hender the huntsman of Lanhydrock and legends of a devil who had played strange pranks with a tower that stands on a neighbouring hill. The notebook in which he had recorded these tales had been lost, and when he returned to recover the tales, the memory had gone from the people and these tales were lost for ever.

Determined that no further 'drolls and romances' should be lost, for ten months he roamed Cornwall and the borders of Dartmoor sitting at the hearths of the country people or in close companionship with the miners, 'drinking deeply from the stream of legendary lore which was at that time flowing as from a well of living water.' He also met possibly the last two wandering story tellers then in Cornwall. Uncle Anthony James was a blind man from Cury who spent his whole year on the road, calling regularly at the same time of year. For a night's lodging and food he would entertain the company with ballads and stories, accompanying himself on the fiddle. The other was Billy Frost of St Just, who used to go the rounds of the feasts in the neighbourhood and be 'well entertained at the public houses for the sake of his drolls'.

Thirty years were to pass between this first collection and the publication of Hunt's work. In that time Hunt established himself as an important scientific writer and a Fellow of the Royal Society, founded a Mechanics' Institute in Plymouth, became a lecturer and later professor at the Royal School of Mines as well as President of the Cornwall Polytechnic Society, and was for 37 years keeper of mining records for the county. In the latter capacity he was able to tour the county, adding to his stock of tales and folk-lore. His most important technical work was *British Mining*, a monumental survey of the industry published in 1884, three years before his death.

Hunt acknowledged the help he received from many people in his compilation of Cornish legends, including William Bottrell who was to publish his own collection in three volumes as *Traditions and Hearthside Stories of West Cornwall*, between 1870 and 1880.

Further selections from Hunt's work can be found in *Customs and Superstitions from Cornish Folklore*, *Cornish Fairies*, *Cornish Folk-lore* and *Demons, Ghosts and Spectres in Cornish Folklore*, all published in this series.

The Giant of the Mount

The history of the redoubtable Jack proves that St Michael's Mount was the abode of the giant Cormelian, or, as the name is sometimes given, Cormoran. We are told how Jack destroyed the giant, and the story ends. Now, the interesting part, which has been forgotten in the narrative, is not only that Cormoran lived on, but that he built the Mount, his dwelling-place. St Michael's Mount, as is tolerably well known, is an island at each rise of the tide – the distance between it and the mainland being a little more than a quarter of a mile. In the days of the giants, however, it was some six miles from the sea, and was known as The White Rock in the wood, or in Cornish, *Carreg luz en kuz*.

In this wood the giant desired to build his home, and to rear it above the trees, that he might from the top keep watch over the neighbouring country. Any person carefully observing the structure of the granite rocks will notice their tendency to a cubical form. These stones were carefully selected by the giant from the granite of the neighbouring hills, and he was for a long period employed in carrying and piling those huge masses, one on the other, in which labour he compelled his wife to aid him. It has been suggested, with much show of probability, that the confusion of the two names alluded to has arisen from the fact that the giant was called Cormoran, and that the name of his wife was Cormelian; at all events, there is no harm in adopting this hypothesis. The toil of lifting those granite masses from their primitive beds, and of carrying them through the forest, was excessive. It would seem that the heaviest burthens were imposed upon Cormelian, and that she was in the habit of carrying those rocky masses in her apron. At a short distance from the White Rock, which was now approaching completion, there exist large masses of greenstone rock. Cormelian saw no reason why one description of stone would not do as well as another; and one day, when the giant Cormoran was sleeping, she broke off a vast mass of the greenstone rock, and taking it in her apron, hastened towards the artificial hill with it, hoping to place it without being observed by

Cormoran. When, however, Cormelian was within a short distance of the White Rock, the giant awoke, and presently perceived that his wife was, contrary to his wishes, carrying a green stone instead of a white one.

In great wrath he arose, followed her, and, with a dreadful imprecation, gave her a kick. Her apron-string broke, and the stone fell on the sand. There it has ever since remained, no human power being sufficient to remove it. The giantess died, and the mass of greenstone, resting, as it does, on clay slate rocks, became her monument. In more recent days, when the light of Christianity was dawning on the land, this famous rock was still rendered sacred: 'a little chapel' having been built on it; and to this day it is usually known as 'The Chapel Rock.'

The Hack and the Cast

In the parish of Goran is an intrenchment running from cliff to cliff, and cutting off about a hundred acres of coarse ground. This is about twenty feet broad, and twenty-four feet high in most places.

Marvellous as it may appear, tradition assures us that this was the work of a giant, and that he performed the task in a single night. This fortification has long been known as *Thica Vosa*, and the Hack and Cast. The giant, who lived on the promontory, was the terror of the neighbourhood, and great were the rejoicings in Goran when his death was accomplished through a stratagem by a neighbouring doctor.

The giant fell ill through eating some food – children or otherwise – to satisfy his voracity, which had disturbed his stomach. His roars and groans were heard for miles, and great was the terror throughout the neighbourhood. A messenger, however, soon arrived at the residence of the doctor of the parish, and he bravely resolved to obey the summons of the giant, and visit him. He found the giant rolling on the ground with pain, and he at once determined to rid the world, if possible, of the monster.

He told him that he must be bled. The giant submitted, and the doctor moreover said that, to insure relief, a large hole in the cliff must be filled with the blood. The giant lay on the ground, his arm extended over the hole, and the blood flowing a torrent into it. Relieved by the loss of blood, he permitted the stream to flow on, until he at last became so weak, that the doctor kicked him over the cliff, and killed him. The well-known promontory of The Dead Man, or Dodman, is so called from the dead giant. The spot on which he fell is the 'Giant's House', and the hole has ever since been most favourable to the growth of ivy.

The Padstow 'Hobby Horse'

At the time of the spring festival, which is observed at Helston as a revel in honour, probably, of Flora, and hence called the 'Furry-day,' and by the blowing of horns and gathering of the 'may' in St Ives and other places, the people of Padstow were a few years since in the habit of riding the 'hobby-horse' to water. This hobby-horse was, after it had been taken round the town, submerged in the sea. The old people said it was once believed that this ceremony preserved the cattle of the inhabitants from disease and death. The appearance of a white horse escaping from the flood which buried the Lyonesse, is told at several points, on both the north and south coast, and the riding of the hobby-horse probably belongs to this tradition. In support of this idea, we must not forget the mermaid story associated with the harbour of Padstow.

The water-horse is a truly Celtic tradition. We have it in the Arabian Nights, and in the stories of all countries in the south of Europe. Mr Campbell in *West Highland Tales*, says he finds the horse brought prominently forward in the Breton legends, and that animal figures largely in traditions of Scotland and Ireland.

Have the miners' phrases 'a horse in the lode', applied to a mass of unproductive ground in the middle of a mineral lode, or, 'Black Jack rides a good horse,' signifying that zinc ore gives good promise for copper, anything to do with these traditions?

The Giants of Trencrom, or Trecrobben

The rough granite hill of Trecrobben rises in almost savage grandeur from the wooded lands which form the park of Trevetha, close by the picturesque village of Lelant. From the summit of this hill may be surveyed one of the most striking panoramic views in Cornwall. The country declines, rather rapidly, but still with a pleasing contour, towards the sea on the southern side. From the sandy plain, which extends from Marazion to Penzance, there stretch out two arms of land, one on the eastern side, towards the Lizard Point, and the other on the western side towards Mousehole and Lamorna, which embrace as it were that fine expanse of water known as the Mount's Bay. The most striking object, 'set in the silver sea', is the pyramidical hill St Michael's Mount, crowned with the 'castle', an unhappy mixture of church, castle, and modern dwelling-house, which, nevertheless, from its very incongruities, has a picturesque appearance when viewed from a distance. Nestling amidst the greenstone rocks, sheltered by 'the Holy Mount', is the irregular town of Marazion, or Market-Jew; and, balancing this, on the western side of 'the Green', Penzance displays her more important buildings, framed by the beautifully fertile country by which the town is surrounded.

The high lands to the westward of Penzance, with the fishing villages of Newlyn and Mousehole, the church of Paul on the summit of the hill, and the engine-house belonging to a mine at its base, have much quiet beauty under some aspects of light – the yet more western hills shutting out the Land's End from the observer's eye.

Looking from Trencrom (this is the more common name) to the south-east, the fine hills of Tregoning and Godolphin – both of which have given names to ancient Cornish families – mark the southern boundary of a district famed for its mineral wealth. Looking eastward, Carn Brea Hill, with its ancient castle and its modern monument, stands up from the tableland in rugged grandeur. This hill, 'a merry place, 'tis said, in days of yore' – when British villages were spread amidst the mighty cairns, and

Cyclopean walls sheltered the inhabitants – rises to mark the most productive piece of mining-ground, of the same area, to be found in the world.

Around the towns of Camborne and Redruth are seen hundreds of miners' cottages, and scores of tall chimneys, telling of the mechanical appliances which are brought to bear upon the extraction of tin and copper from the earth. Beyond this thickly-peopled region the eye wanders yet eastwards and eventually reposes on the series of granite hills which rise beyond St Austell and stretch northward, the two highest hills in Cornwall, which are known as Roughtor and Brownwilly, being in this range.

Let the observer now turn his face northward, and a new and varied scene lies before him. Within two miles the waters of St Ives Bay break against the cliffs. On the left is the creek of Hayle, which has been fashioned by the energy of man into a useful harbour, and given rise to the foundation of two extensive iron-foundries. Between those and the sea are the hills of blown sand, which have ever been the homes of the Fairy people.

The lighthouse of Godrevy stands, a humble companion, to balance in this bay the Mount, which adorns the bay, washing the southern slope of this narrow neck of land. Godrevy marks the region of sand extending to the eastward. To the north the shores become more and more rugged, culminating in St Agnes' Beacon – a hill of graceful form rising somewhat rapidly to a considerable elevation. From this the 'beetling cliffs' stretch away northward, until the bold promontory Trevose Head closes the scene, appropriately displaying another of those fine examples of humanity – a lighthouse.

To the left, towards the sea, rises the cenotaph of Knill, an eccentric man, who evidently sought to secure some immortality by this building and the silly ceremonials carried on around it, the due performance of which he has secured by bequests to the Corporation of St Ives. Around this the mining district of St Ives is seen, and her fishing-boats dotting the sea give evidence of another industry of vast importance to the town and neighbourhood. Westward of St

Ives, hills more brown and rugged than any which have yet been viewed stretch away to Zennor, Morva, and St Just, and these, girding the scene beneath our feet, shut out from us the region of the Land s End.

On the summit of this hill, which is only surpassed in savage grandeur by Carn Brea, the giants built a castle – the four entrances to which still remain in Cyclopean massiveness to attest the Herculean powers by which such mighty blocks were piled upon each other. There the giant chieftains dwelt in awful state. Along the serpentine road, passing up the hill to the principal gateway, they dragged their captives, and on the great flat rocks within the castle they sacrificed them. Almost every rock still bears some name connected with the giants – 'a race may perish, but the name endures'. The treasures of the giants who dwell here are said to have been buried in the days of their troubles when they were perishing before the conquerors of their land. Their gold and jewels were hidden deep in the granite caves of this hill, and secured by spells as potent as those which Merlin placed upon his hoarded treasures. They are securely preserved even to the present day, and carefully guarded from man by the Spriggans, or Trolls.

The Fairy Fair in Germoe

Bal Lane in Germoe was a notorious place for piskies. One night Daniel Champion and his comrade came to Godolphin Bridge; they were a little bit 'overtook' with liquor. They said that when they came to Bal Lane, they found it covered all over from end to end, and the Small People holding a fair there with all sorts of merchandise – the prettiest sight they ever met with. Champion was sure he saw his child there; for a few nights before, his child in the evening was as beautiful a one as could be seen anywhere, but in the morning was changed for one as ugly and wizened as could be; and he was sure the Small People had done it. Next day, telling the story at Croft Gothal, his comrade was knocked backward, thrown into the bob-pit, and just killed. Obliged to be carried to his home, Champion followed and was telling of their adventure with the

Small People, when one said, 'Don't speak about them; they're wicked, spiteful devils.' No sooner were the words uttered than the speaker was thrown clean over stairs and bruised dreadfully – a convincing proof to all present of the reality of the existence of the Small Folks.

The rival giants

Those have visited the Logan Rock will be familiar with the several groups which form the Treryn promontory. Treryn Castle, an ancient British fortress, the Cyclopean walls of which, and its outer earthwork, can still be traced, was the dwelling of a famous giant and his wife. I have heard it said that he gave his name to this place, but that is, of course, doubtful. This giant was chief of a numerous band, and by his daring he held possession, against the giants of the Mount, of all the lands west of Penzance. Amongst the hosts who owed allegiance to him was a remarkable fine young fellow, who had his abode in a cave, in the pile of rocks upon which the Logan Rock stands. This young giant grew too fond of the giantess, and it would appear that the lady was not unfavourably inclined towards him. Of their love passes, however, we know nothing. Tradition has only told us that the giantess was one day reclining on the rock still known as the Giant Lady's Chair, while the good old giant was dosing in the Giant's Chair which stands near it, when the young and wicked lover stole behind his chief and stabbed him in the belly with a knife. The giant fell over the rocks to the level ridge below, and there he lay, rapidly pouring out his life-blood. From this spot the young murderer kicked him into the sea, ere yet his life was quite extinct, and he perished in the waters.

The guilty pair took possession of Treryn Castle, and, we are told, lived happily for many years.

Jago's demon

The vicar of Wendron, who bore the name of Jago, appears to have had strange intercourse with the invisible world; or, rather, the primitive people of this district believe him to have possessed supernatural powers. Any one visiting the parish of Wendron will be struck with many distinguishing features in its inhabitants. It would appear as if a strange people had settled down amidst the races already inhabiting the spot, and that they had studiously avoided any intimate connection with their neighbours. The dialect of the Wendron people is unlike any other in Cornwall, and there are many customs existing amongst them which are not found in any other part of the county.

Until of late years, the inhabitants of Wendron were quite uneducated – hence the readiness with which they associate ancient superstitions with comparatively modern individuals.

The Reverend Mr Jago was no doubt a man who impressed this people with the powers of his knowledge. Hence we are told that no spirit walking the earth could resist the spells laid upon him by Jago. By his prayers – or powers – many a night wanderer has been put back into his grave, and so confined that the poor ghost could never again get loose. To the evil-disposed, Mr Jago was a terror. All Wendron believed that every act was visible to the parson at the moment it was done – day or night it mattered not. He has been known to pick a thief at once out of a crowd, and criminal men or women could not endure the glance of his eye. Many a person has at once confessed to guilty deeds of which they have been suspected the moment they have been brought before Mr Jago.

We are told that he had spirits continually waiting upon him, though invisible until he desired them to appear. The parson rode far and wide over the moorland of his parish. He never took a groom with him; for, the moment he alighted from his horse, he had only to strike the earth with his whip, and up came a demongroom to take charge of the steed.

The phantom ship

Years long ago, one night, a gig's crew was called to go off to a 'hobble', to the westwards of St Ives Head. No sooner was one boat launched than several others were put off from the shore, and a stiff chase was maintained, each one being eager to get to the ship, as she had the appearance of a foreign trader. The hull was clearly visible: she was a schooner-rigged vessel, with a light over her bows.

Away they pulled, and the boat which had been first launched still kept ahead by dint of mechanical power and skill. All the men had thrown off their jackets to row with more freedom. At length the helmsman cried out, 'Stand ready to board her.' The sailor rowing the bow oar slipped it out of the row-lock, and stood on the forethought, taking his jacket on his arm, ready to spring aboard.

The vessel came so close to the boat that they could see the men, and the bow-oar man made a grasp at her bulwarks. His hand found nothing solid, and he fell, being caught by one of his mates, back into the boat, instead of into the water. Then ship and lights disappeared. The next morning the *Neptune* of London, Captain Richard Grant, was wrecked at Gwithian, and all perished. The captain's body was picked up after a few days, and that of his son also. They were both buried in Gwithian churchyard.

The giants at play

In Cornwall there are evidences that these Titans were a sportive race. Huge rocks are preserved to show where they played at trap-ball, at hurling, and other athletic games. The giants of Trecrobben and St Michael's Mount often met for a game at bob-buttons. The Mount was the 'bob,' on which flat masses of granite were placed to serve as buttons, and Trecrobben Hill was the 'mit', or the spot from which the throw was made. This order was sometimes reversed. On the outside of St Michael's Mount, many a granite slab which had been knocked off the 'bob' is yet to be found; and numerous piles of rough cubical masses of the same rock, said to be the granite of Trecrobben Hill, show how eagerly the game was played.

Trecrobben Hill was well chosen by the giants as the site of their castle. From it they surveyed the country on every side; and friend or enemy was seen at a considerable distance as he approached the guarded spot. It is as clear as tradition can make it, that Trecrobben was the centre of a region full of giants. On Lescudjack Hill, close to Penzance, there is 'The Giant's Round,' evidently the scene of many a sanguinary conflict, since the Cornish antiquarian authority Borlase informs us, that *Lesgudzhek* signifies the 'Castle of the Bloody Field'. On the cairn at Gulval are several impressions on the rocks, all referable to the giants. In Madron there is the celebrated 'Giant's Cave'; and the well known Lanyon cromlech is reported by some to be the 'Giant's Coit,' while others declare it to be the 'Giant's Table'. Cairn Galva, again, is celebrated for its giant; and, indeed, every hill within sight has some monument preserving the memory of 'the Titans fierce'.

The mermaid of Seaton

Near Looe – that is, between Down Derry and Looe – there is a little sand-beach called Seaton. Tradition tells us that here once stood a goodly commercial town bearing this name, and that when it was in its pride, Plymouth was but a small fishing-village.

The town of Seaton is said to have been overwhelmed with sand at an early period, the catastrophe having been brought about – as in the case of the filling up of Padstow harbour – by the curse of a mermaid, who had suffered some injury from the sailors who belonged to this port. Beyond this I have been unable to glean any story worth preserving.

The witch and the toad

An old woman called Alsey – usually Aunt Alsey – occupied a small cottage in Anthony, one of a row which belonged to a tradesman living in Dock – as Devonport was then designated, to distinguish it from Plymouth. The old woman possessed a very violent temper, and this, more than anything else, fixed upon her the character of being a witch.

Her landlord had frequently sought his rent, and just as frequently he received nothing but abuse. He had, on the occasion to which our narrative refers, crossed the Tamar and walked to Anthony, with the firm resolve of securing his rent, now long in arrear, and of turning the old termagant out of the cottage. A violent scene ensued, and the vicious old woman, more than a match for a really kind-hearted and quiet man, remained the mistress of the situation. She seated herself in the door of her cottage and cursed her landlord's wife, 'the child she was carrying', and all belonging to him, with so devilish a spite that Mr — owned he was fairly driven away in terror.

On returning home, he, of course, told his wife all the circumstances; and while they were discoursing on the subject – the whole story being attentively listened to by their daughter, then a young girl, who is now my informant – a woman came into the shop requiring some articles which they sold. 'Sit still, father,' said Mrs — to her husband; 'you must be tired. I will see to the shop.' So she went from the parlour into the shop, and, hearing the wants of her customer, proceeded to supply them; gossiping gaily, as was her wont, to interest the buyer. Mrs — was weighing one of the articles required when something falling heavily from the ceiling of the shop struck the beam out of her hand, and both – the falling body and scales – came together with much noise on to the counter. At the same instant both women screamed, the shop-keeper calling also 'Father! father!' – meaning her husband thereby – with great energy.

Mr — and his daughter were in the shop instantly, and there, on the counter, they saw an enormous and most ugly toad sprawling amidst the chains of the scales. The first action of the man was to turn back to the parlour, seize the tongs, and return to the shop. He grasped the swollen toad with the tongs, the vicious creature spitting all the time, and, without a word, he went back and flung it behind the block of wood which was burning in the grate. The object of terror being removed, the wife, who was shortly to become the mother of another child, though usually a woman who had great command over her feelings, fainted.

This circumstance demanding all their attention, the toad was forgotten. The shock was a severe one; and although Mrs — was restored in a little time to her senses, she again and again became faint.

Those fits continuing, her medical attendant, Dr — was sent for, and on his arrival he ordered that his patient should be immediately placed in bed, and the husband was informed that he must be prepared for a premature birth.

The anxiety occasioned by these circumstances, and the desire to afford every relief to his wife, so fully occupied Mr —, that for an hour or two he entirely forgot the cause of all this mischief; or, perhaps satisfying himself that the toad was burnt to ashes, he had no curiosity to look after it. He was, however, suddenly summoned from the bedroom, in which he was with his wife, by his daughter calling to him, in a voice of terror:

'O father, the toad, the toad!'

Mr — rushed downstairs, and he then discovered that the toad, though severely burnt, had escaped destruction. It must have crawled up over the log of wood, and from it have fallen down amongst the ashes. There it was now making useless struggles to escape, by climbing over the fender.

The tongs were again put in requisition, with the intention this time of carrying the reptile out of the house. Before, however, he had time to do so, a man from Anthony came hastily into the shop with the information that Aunt Alsey had fallen into the fire, as the people supposed, in a fit, and that she was nearly burnt to death. This man had been sent off with two commissions – one to fetch the doctor, and the other to bring Mr — with him, as much of the cottage had been injured by fire, communicated to it by the old woman's dress.

In as short a time as possible the parish surgeon and Mr — were at Anthony and too truly they found the old woman most severely burnt – so seriously, indeed, there was no chance that one so aged could rally from the shock which her system must have received. However, a litter was carefully prepared, the old woman was placed in it, and carried to the workhouse. Every attention was given to her situation, but she never recovered perfect consciousness, and during the night she died.

The toad, which we left inside the fender in front of a blazing fire, was removed from a position so trying to any cold-blooded animal, by the servant, and thrown, with a 'hugh' and a shudder, upon one of the flower-beds in the small garden behind the house.

There it lay the next morning, dead, and when examined by Mr —, it was found that all the injuries sustained by the toad corresponded with those received by the poor old wretch, who had no doubt fallen a victim to passion.

As we have only to deal with the mysterious relation which existed between the witch and the toad, it is not necessary that we should attend further to the innocent victim of an old woman's vengeance, than to say that eventually a babe was born – that that babe grew to be a handsome man, was an officer in the navy, and having married, went to sea, and perished, leaving a widow with an unborn child to lament his loss. Whether this was a result of the witch's curse, those who are more deeply skilled in witchcraft than I am may perhaps tell.

The giant Bolster

This mighty man held especial possession of the hill formerly known as Carne Bury-anacht or Bury-allack, 'the sparstone grave,' and sometimes called 'St Agnes' Ball' and 'St Agnes' Pestis', but which is now named, from the use made of the hill during the long war, St Agnes' Beacon. He has left his name to a very interesting, and undoubtedly most ancient earthwork, which still exists at the base of the hill, and evidently extended from Trevaunance Porth as far as Chapel Porth, enclosing the most important tin district in St Agnes. This is constantly called 'The Bolster'.

Bolster must have been of enormous size; since it is stated that he could stand with one foot on St Agnes' Beacon and the other on Carn Brea; these hills being distant, as the bird flies, six miles, his immensity will be clear to all. In proof of this, there still exists, in the valley running upwards from Chapel Porth, a stone in which may yet be seen the impression of the giant's fingers. On one occasion, Bolster, when enjoying his usual stride from the Beacon to Carn Brea, felt thirsty, and stooped to drink out of the well at Chapel Porth, resting, while he did so, on the stone.

We hear but little of the wives of our giants; but Bolster had a wife, who was made to labour hard by her tyrannical husband. On the top of St Agnes' Beacon there yet exist the evidences of the useless labours to which this unfortunate giantess was doomed, in grouped masses of small stones. These, it is said, have all been gathered from an estate at the foot of the hill, immediately adjoining the village of St Agnes. This farm is to the present day remarkable for its freedom from stones, though situated amidst several others, which, like most lands reclaimed from the moors of this district, have stones in abundance mixed with the soil. Whenever Bolster was angry with his wife, he compelled her to pick stones, and to carry them in her apron to the top of the hill.

There is some confusion in the history of this giant, and of the blessed St Agnes to whom the church is dedicated. They are supposed to have lived at the same time, which, according to our views, is scarcely probable, believing, as we do, that no giants existed long after their defeat at Plymouth by Brutus and Corineus. There may have been an earlier saint of the same name; or may not Saint Enns or Anns, the popular name of this parish, indicate some other lady?

Be this as it may, the giant Bolster became deeply in love with St Agnes, who is reputed to have been singularly beautiful, and a pattern woman of virtue. The giant allowed the lady no repose. He followed her incessantly, proclaiming his love, and filling the air with the tempests of his sighs and groans. St Agnes lectured Bolster in vain on the impropriety of his conduct, he being already a married man. This availed not; her prayers to him to relieve her from his importunities were also in vain. The persecuted lady finding there was no release for her, while this monster existed, resolved to be rid of him at any cost, and eventually succeeded by the following stratagem: Agnes appeared at length to be persuaded of the intensity of the giant's love, but she told him she required yet one small proof more. There exists at Chapel Porth a hole in the cliff at the termination of the valley. If Bolster would fill this hole with his blood the lady would no longer look coldly on him.

This huge bestrider-of-the-hills thought that it was an easy thing which was required of him, and felt that he could fill many such holes and be none the weaker for the loss of blood. Consequently, stretching his great arm across the hole, he plunged a knife into a vein, and a torrent of gore issued forth. Roaring and seething the blood fell to the bottom, and the giant expected in a few minutes to see the test of his devotion made evident, in the filling of the hole. It required much more blood than Bolster had supposed; still it must in a short time be filled, so he bled on. Hour after hour the blood flowed from the vein, yet the hole was not filled. Eventually the giant fainted from exhaustion. The strength of life within his mighty frame enabled him to rally, yet he had no power to lift himself from the ground, and he was unable to stanch the wound which he had made. Thus it was, that after many throes, the giant Bolster died!

The cunning saint, in proposing this task to Bolster, was well aware that the hole opened at the bottom into the sea, and that as rapidly as the blood flowed into the hole it ran from it, and did

> The multitudinous seas incarnadine,
> Making the green one red.

Thus the lady got rid of her hated lover; Mrs Bolster was released, and the district freed from the presence of a tyrant. The hole at Chapel Porth still retains the evidences of the truth of this tradition, in the red stain which marks the track down which flowed the giant's blood.

Kenidzhek witch

On the tract called the 'Gump' near Kenidzhek is a beautiful well of clear water, not far from which was a miner's cot, in which dwelt two miners with their sister. They told her never to go to the well after dark; they would fetch the water for her. However, on one Saturday night she had forgotten to get in a supply for the morrow, so she went off to the well. Passing by a gap in a broken-down hedge (called a gurgo) near the well, she saw an old woman sitting down, wrapped in a red shawl; she asked her what she did there at that time of night, but received no reply; she thought this rather strange, but plunged her pitcher in the well. When she drew it up, though a perfectly sound vessel, it contained no water; she tried again and again, and though she saw the water rushing in at the mouth of the pitcher, it was sure to be empty when lifted out. She then became rather frightened, spoke again to the old woman, but receiving no answer, hastened away, and came in great alarm to her brothers. They told her that it was on account of this old woman they did not wish her to go to the well at night. What she saw was the ghost of old Moll, a witch who had been a great terror to the people in her lifetime, and had laid many fearful spells on them. They said they saw her sitting in the gap by the wall every night when going to bed.

The legend of Tamara

The lovely nymph Tamara was born in a cavern. Although her parents were spirits of the earth, the child loved the light of day. Often had they chided her for yielding to her desires and visiting the upper world; and often had they warned her against the consequences which would probably arise from her neglect of their advice. The giants of the moors were to be feared; and it was from these that the earth spirits desired to protect their child.

Tamara – beautiful, young, heedless – never lost an opportunity of looking on the glorious sun. Two sons of Dartmoor giants – Tavy and Tawrage – had seen the fair maid, and longed to possess her. Long was their toil, and the wild maiden often led them over mountain and moor in playful chase.

Under a bush in Morewinstow, one day, both Tavy and Tawrage came upon Tamara. They resolved now to compel her to declare upon which of them her choice should fall. The young men used every persuasion, and called her by every endearing name. Her parents had missed Tamara, and they sought and found her seated between the sons of the giants whom they hated. The gnome father caused a deep sleep to fall on the eye of Tavy and Tawrage, and then he endeavoured to persuade his daughter to return to his subterranean cell.

Tamara would not leave her lovers. In his rage, the gnome cursed his daughter and, by the might of his curse, changed her into a river, which should flow on for ever to the salt sea. The lovely Tamara dissolved in tears, and as a crystal stream of exceeding beauty the waters glided onward to the ocean.

At length Tavy awoke. His Tamara was gone; he fled to his father in the hills. The giant knew of the metamorphosis, and, to ease the anguish of his son, he transformed him into a stream. Rushing over rocks, running through morasses, gliding along valleys, and murmuring amidst the groves, Tavy still goes on seeking for Tamara – his only joy being that he runs by her side and that, mingling their waters, they glide together to the eternal sea.

Tawrage awakened after a long sleep. He divined what had taken place, and fled to the hills to an enchanter. At his prayer he, too, was changed to a stream; but he mistook the road along which Tamara had gone, and onward, ever sorrowing, he flows away-away-away from his Tamara for ever. Thus originated the Tamar, the Tavy, and the Taw.

The fairy miners – the knockers

At Ransom Mine the Knockers were always very active in their subterranean operations. In every part of the mine their knockings were heard, but most especially were they busy in one particular 'end'. There was a general impression that great wealth must exist at this part of the lode. Yet, notwithstanding that inducements of very high 'tribute' were held out to the miners, no pair of men could be found brave enough to venture on the ground of the 'Bockles'.

An old man and his son, called Trenwith, who lived near Bosprenis, went out one midsummer eve, about midnight, and watched until they saw the 'Smae People' bringing up the shining ore. It is said they were possessed of some secret by which they could communicate with the fairy people. Be this as it may, they told the little miners that they would save them all the trouble of breaking down the ore, that they would bring 'to grass' for them, one-tenth of the 'richest stuff' and leave it properly dressed, if they would quietly give them up this end. An agreement of some kind was come to. The old man and his son took the 'pitch', and in a short time realised much wealth. The old man never failed to keep to his bargain, and leave the tenth of the ore for his friends. He died. The son was avaricious and selfish. He sought to cheat the Knockers, but he ruined himself by so doing. The 'lode' failed; nothing answered with him; disappointed, he took to drink, squandered all the money his father had made, and died a beggar.

The great Wrath or Ralph

Not far from Portreath there exists a remarkable fissure, or gorge, on the coast, formed by the wearing out, through the action of the sea, of a channel of ground softer than that which exists on either side of it. This is generally known as Ralph's Cupboard; and one tale is that Ralph was a famous smuggler, who would run his little vessel, even in dark nights, into the shelter afforded by this gorge, and safely land his goods. Another is, that it was formerly a cavern in which dwelt Wrath – a huge giant, who was the terror of the fishermen. Sailing from St Ives, they ever avoided the Cupboard; as they said, 'Nothing ever came out of it which was unfortunate enough to get into it.' Wrath is reputed to have watched for those who were drifted towards his Cupboard by currents, or driven in by storms. It is said that wading out to sea, he tied the boats to his girdle, and quietly walked back to his den, making, of course, all the fishermen his prey. The roof of the cavern is supposed to have fallen in after the death of the giant, leaving the open chasm as we now see it.

Morva or Morveth

The parish of this name is situated on the north-west coast of Cornwall, the parish of St Just being on its western borders, and that of Zennor on the east, between it and St Ives. The Cornish historian Tonkin says, 'Morva signifies *Locus Maritimus*, a place near the sea, as this parish is. The name is sometimes written Morveth, implying much the same sense.'

The similarity of this name to 'Morgan,' sea-women, and 'Morverch,' sea-daughters, which Mr Keightley has shown us is applied to the mermaids of the Breton ballads, is not a little curious. There are several stories current in this parish of ladies seen on the rocks, of ladies going off from the shore to peculiar isolated rocks at special seasons, and of ladies sitting weeping and wailing on the shore.

Mr Blight, in his *Week at the Land's End*, speaking of the church in the adjoining parish of Zennor, which still remains in nearly its primitive condition whereas Morva church is a modern structure, says: 'Some of the bench ends were carved; on one is a strange figure of a mermaid, which to many might seem out of character in a church.' (Mr Blight gives a drawing of this bench end.) This is followed by a quotation bearing the initials R.S.H., which, it is presumed, are those of the Rev. R.S.Hawker, of Morwenstow:

The fishermen who were the ancestors of the Church, came from the Galilean waters to haul for men. We, born to God at the font, are children of the water. Therefore, all the early symbolism of the Church was of and from the sea. The carvure of the early arches was taken from the sea and its creatures. Fish, dolphins, mermen, and mermaids abound in the early types, transferred to wood and stone.

Surely the poet of 'the Western Shore' might have explained the fact of the figures of mermaids being carved on the bench ends of some of the old churches with less difficulty, had he remembered that nearly all the churches on the coast of Cornwall were built by and for fishermen, to whom the superstitions of mermen and mermaidens had the familiarity of a creed.

The intimate connection between the inhabitants of Brittany, of Cornwall, and of Wales, would appear to lead to the conclusion that the Breton word *morverch*, or mermaid, had much to do with the name of this parish, Morva, of Morvel, near Liskeard, and probably of Morwenstow, of which the vicar, Mr Hawker, writes:

'My glebe occupies a position of wild and singular beauty. Its western boundary is the sea, skirted by tall and tremendous cliffs, and near their brink, with the exquisite taste of ecclesiastical antiquity, is placed the church. The original and proper designation of the parish is Morwen-stow – that is, Morwenna's Stow, or station; but it has been corrupted by recent usage, like many other local names.'

The mermaid of Padstow

The port of Padstow has a good natural harbour so far as rocky area goes, but it is so choked up with drifting sands as to be nearly useless. A peasant recently thus explained the cause. He told how 'it was once deep water for the largest vessel, and under the care of a merry-maid' – as he called her; but one day, as she was sporting on the surface, a fellow with a gun shot at her. 'She dived for a moment; but re-appearing, raised her right arm, and vowed that henceforth the harbour should be desolate. And,' added the old man, 'it always will be so. We have had commissions, and I know not what, about converting this place into a harbour of refuge. A harbour of refuge would be a great blessing, but not all the Government commissions in the world could keep the sand out, or make the harbour deep enough to swim a frigate, unless the parsons can find out the way to take up the merry-maid's curse.'

The devil's doorway

In the slate (killas) formations behind Polperro is a good example of a fault. The geologist, in the pride of his knowledge, refers this to some movement of the solid mass – a rending of the rocks, produced either by the action of some subterranean force lifting the earth-crust, or by a depression of one division of the rocks. The wisdom of our grandfathers led them to a conclusion widely different from this.

The mighty ruler of the realms of darkness, who is known to have an especial fondness for rides at midnight, 'to see how his little ones thrive,' ascending from his subterranean country, chose this spot as his point of egress.

As he rose from below in his fiery car, drawn by a gigantic jet black steed, the rocks gave way before him, and the rent at Polperro remains to this day to convince all unbelievers. Not only this, as his Satanic majesty burst through the slate rocks, his horse, delighted with the airs of this upper world, reared in wild triumph, and, planting again his hoof upon the ground, made these islands shake as with an earthquake; and he left the deep impression of his burning foot behind. There, any unbeliever may see the hoof-shaped pool, unmistakable evidence of the wisdom of the days gone by.

The witches of the logan stone

Who that has travelled into Cornwall but has visited the Logan Stone? Numerous logan rocks exist on the granite hills of the county, but that remarkable mass which is poised on the cubical masses forming its Cyclopean support, at Trereen, is beyond all others the Logan Stone.

A more sublime spot could not have been chosen by the Bardic priesthood for any ordeal connected with their worship; and even admitting that nature may have disposed the huge mass to wear away, so as to rest delicately poised on a pivot, it is highly probable that the wild worship of the untrained tribes, who had passed to these islands from the shores of the Mediterranean Sea, may have led them to believe that some superhuman power belonged to such a strangely-balanced mass of rock.

Nothing can be more certain than that through all time, passing on from father to son, there has been a wild reverence of this mass of rock; and long after the days when the Druid ceased to be there is every reason for believing that the Christian priests, if they did not encourage, did not forbid the use of this and similar rocks to be used as places of ordeal by the uneducated and superstitious people around.

Hence the mass of rock on which is poised the Logan Stone has ever been connected with the supernatural. To the south of the

Logan Rock is a high peak of granite, towering above the other rocks; this is known as the Castle Peak.

No one can say for how long a period, but most certainly for ages, this peak has been the midnight rendezvous for witches. Many a man, and woman too, now sleeping quietly in the church-yard of St Levan, would, had they the power, attest to have seen the witches flying into the Castle Peak on moonlit nights, moun-ted on the stems of the ragwort and bringing with them the things necessary to make their charms potent and strong.

This place was long noted as the gathering place of the army of witches who took their departure for Wales, where they would lux-uriate at the most favoured seasons of the year upon the milk of the Welshmen's cows. From this peak many a struggling ship has been watched by a malignant crone, while she has been brewing the tempest to destroy it; and many a rejoicing chorus has been echoed, in horror, by the cliffs around, when the witches have been croaking their miserable delight over the perishing crews, as they have watched man, woman and child drowning, whom they were presently to rob of the treasures they were bringing home from other lands.

Upon the rocks behind the Logan Rock it would appear that every kind of mischief which can befall man or beast was once brewed by the St Levan witches.

The horns on the church tower

When the masons were building the tower of Towednack Church, the devil came every night and carried off the pinnacles and battle-ments. Again and again this work was renewed during the day, and as often it was removed during the night, until at length the builders gave up the work in despair, feeling that it was of no use to contend with the evil one.

Thus it was that Towednack Church stands lonely, with its squat and odd-looking tower, a mark of the power of evil to the present day. Associated with this tower is a proverb: 'There are no cuckolds in Towednack, because there are no horns of the church tower.'

The mutton feast

An old tradition – the particulars of which I have failed to recover – says that a flock of sheep were blown from the Gwithian Sands over into St Ives Bay, and that the St Ives fishermen caught them, believing them to be a new variety of fish, either in their nets, or with hook and line, and brought them ashore as their night's catch.

The Lizard people

There is a tradition that the Lizard people were formerly a very inferior race. In fact it is said that they went on all fours, till the crew of a foreign vessel, wrecked on the coast, settled among them, and improved the race so much that they became as remarkable for their stature and physical development as they had been before for the reverse. At this time, as a whole, the Lizard folks certainly have among them a very large population of tall people, many of the men and women being over six feet in height.

The spectre ship of Porthcurno

Porthcurno Cove is situated a little to the west of the Logan Stone. There, as in nearly all the coves around the coast, there once existed a small chapel or oratory, which appears to have been dedicated to St Leven. There exists now a little square enclosure about the size of a sheep's house, which is all that remains of this holy place. Looking up the valley, you may see a few trees, with the chimney tops and part of the roof of an old-fashioned house. That place is Raftra, where they say St Leven church was to have been built; but as fast as the stones were taken there by day, they were removed by night to the place of the present church. (These performances are usually the act of the devil, but I have no information as to the saint or sinner who did this work.) Raftra House, at the time it was built, was the largest mansion west of Penzance. It is said to have been erected by the Tresillians, and, ere it was finished, they were obliged to sell house and lands for less than it had cost them to build the house.

This valley is, in every respect, a melancholy spot, and during a period of storms or at night it is exactly the place which might well be haunted by demon revellers. In the days of the saint from whom the parish has its name, St Leven, he lived a long way from the cove, at a place called Bodelan, and his influence made that, which is now so dreary, a garden. By his pure holiness he made the wilderness a garden of flowers, and spread gladness where now is desolation. Few persons cared to cross that valley after nightfall; and it is not more than thirty years since that I had a narrative from an inhabitant of Penberth, that he himself had seen the spectre ship sailing over the land.

This strange apparition is said to have been observed frequently, coming in from sea about nightfall, when the mists were rising from the marshy ground in the Bottoms.

Onward came the ill-omened craft. It passed steadily through the breakers on the shore, glided up over the sands, and steadily pursued its course over the dry land, as if it had been water. She is described to have been a black, square-rigged, single-masted affair, usually, but not always, followed by a boat. No crew was ever seen. It is supposed they were below, and that the hatches were battened down. On it went to Bodelan, where St Leven formerly dwelt. It would then steer its course to Chygwiden, and there vanish like smoke.

Many of the old people have seen this ship, and no one ever saw it, upon whom some bad luck was not sure to fall.

This ship is somehow connected with a strange man who returned from sea, and went to live at Chygwiden. It may be five hundred years since, it may be but fifty.

He was accompanied by a servant of foreign and forbidding aspect, who continued to be his only attendant, and this servant was never known to speak to any one save his master. It is said by some that they were pirates; others make them more familiar, by calling them privateers; while some insist upon it they were American buccaneers. Whatever they may have been, there was but little seen of them by any of their neighbours. They kept a boat at Porthcurno Cove, and at daylight they would start for sea, never returning until night, and not infrequently remaining out the whole of the night, especially if the weather was tempestuous. This kind of sea-life was varied by hunting. It mattered not to them whether it was day or night; when the storm was loudest, there was this strange man, accompanied either by his servant or by the devil, and the midnight cry of his dogs would disturb the country.

This mysterious being died, and then the servant sought the aid of a few of the peasantry to bear his coffin to the churchyard. The corpse was laid in the grave, around which the dogs were gathered, with the foreigner in their midst. As soon as the earth was thrown on the coffin, man and dogs disappeared, and, strange to say, the boat disappeared at the same moment from the cove. It has never since been seen; and from that day to this, no one has been able to keep a boat in Porthcurno Cove.

The Nine Maids, or Virgin Sisters

Nine 'moor stones' are set up near the road in the parish of Gwendron, or Wendron, to which the above name is given. The perpendicular blocks of granite have evidently been placed with much labour in their present position. Tradition says they indicate the graves of nine sisters. Hals appears to think some nuns were buried here. From one person only I heard the old story of the stones having been metamorphosed maidens.

Other groups of stone might be named in the west, as Rosemedery, Tregaseal, Boskednan, Botallack, Tredinek, and Crowlas, to which the same story extends, and others in the eastern parts of the county.

The giant of Nancledry

In Nancledry Bottoms, about a mile from the famous hill Castle-an-Dinas, there stood at one time a thatched house near the brook which runs murmuring down the valley. Rather more than thirty years since, some mouldering 'clob' (mud) walls, indicating the existence at one time of a large dwelling, were pointed to as the former residence of a terrible giant. He appears to have led a solitary life, and to have lived principally on little children, whom he is said to have swallowed whole. His strength was indicated by several huge masses of granite which were scattered around the Bottoms, and in the neighbouring fields. These were carried by him in his pockets, to defend himself from the giants of Trecrobben. This giant is noteworthy as the only one recorded who lived in a house.

The Garrack Zans

A few years – really but a few years – since, the stone altars on which the first inhabitants of these islands lit their holy fires had yet a place amongst us. In the village of Roskestall stood one such altar; in Treen was to be found another. These huge masses of rock, rendered sacred by the memories surrounding them, have been wantonly removed, and employed in most cases in furnishing pillars at the 'grand entrances' of the houses of the squire farmers of the Land's End district; or they have been yet more rudely served, and are to be found at the entrance to a pigsty, or in the gate-posts to a potato-field.

The extinction of several of the old families is, to the present day, ascribed by the peasantry to the unholy act of removing or breaking up of the Garrick Zans in the village of Escols. The rock in the village of Mayon was called indifferently *table-mayon* (men), or the Garrack Zans. Within our memory is the gathering of the villagers around the Holy Rock. It was their custom, when anything was stolen, or a misdemeanour committed, to light a fire on this altar, and when the fagots were in full blaze, all those who sought to prove their innocence took a burning stick from the rock and spat on the blazing end. If they could extinguish the fire by spitting on the stick, they were declared innocent; but if their mouth was so dry as not to generate sufficient moisture to be heard 'frizzing' on it, that unfortunate individual was suspected, if not declared, to be guilty.

The Midsummer bonfire was first lighted on the rock in Escols, next on the Chapel Hill; then all the other beacon hills were soon ablaze. Many superstitious rites were formerly performed on the

Garrack Zans, which are only found now as the amusements of young people on the eves of St Agnes and Midsummer.

Peter the Devil

The church at Altarnun is said to have been built from the remains of an ancient nunnery which had been founded in the early days of Christianity by the saint to whom it was dedicated.

There was a peculiar sanctity about all that surrounded this little church and its holy well, and few were unfaithful enough to scoff at any of the holy traditions of the sacred place.

About the time of Charles II, an under-clerk or deacon of this church was called Peter, and he is said to have been a man of exceedingly bad character. He scoffed at holy things, and – unless he was belied – he made use of his position for merely temporal benefit, and was not remarkable for his honesty. He was, moreover, the terror of the neighbourhood. Common report insisting on it that Peter had been known to disentomb the dead, whether for the purpose of stealing rings and other trinkets which may have been buried, as some said, or for the purpose of renewing his youth, as others suggested, by mysterious contact with the dead, was not clearly made out. He was invariably called Peter Jowle, or Joule – that is, Peter the Devil. At the age of a hundred he was a gray-headed, toothless man; but then, by some diabolical incantation, he is said to have caused new black hairs to spring forth amongst those which were white with age, and then also new teeth grew in his jaws. Peter is said to have died when he was more than a hundred and fifty years old.

Christmas Eve in the mines

On Christmas Eve, in former days, the small people, or the spriggans, would meet at the bottom of the deepest mines, and have a midnight mass. Then those who were in the mine would hear voices, melodious beyond all earthly voices, singing, 'Now well! now well'; and the strains of some deep-toned organ would shake the rocks.

Of the grandeur of those meetings, old stories could not find words sufficiently sonorous to speak; it was therefore left to the imagination. But this was certain, the temple formed by the fairy bands in which to celebrate the eve of the birth of a Saviour, in whose mercy they all had hope, was of the most magnificent description.

Midsummer-eve and New-year's day and eve are holidays with the miners. It has been said they refuse to work on those days from superstitious reasons. I never heard of any.

The cock-crow stone

A rock of white marble (?) with many rock basins on its surface lies in Looe harbour, under Saunder's Lane, and is now covered by every tide. This stone once stood on the top of an elevated rock near it, and when in this position, whenever it heard a cock crow in the neighbouring farmyard of Hay, it turned round three times.

The topmost stone of that curious pile of rocks in the parish of St Cleer known as the Cheesewring is gifted in like manner.

How Pengerswick became a sorcerer

The first Pengerswick, by whom the castle, which still bears his name, was built, was a proud man, and desired to ally himself with some of the best families of Cornwall. He wished his son to wed a lady who was very much older than himself, who is said to have been connected with the Godolphin family. This elderly maiden had a violent desire either for the young man or the castle – it is not very clear which. The young Pengerswick gave her no return for the manifestations of love which she lavished upon him. Eventually, finding that all her attempts to win the young man's love were abortive, and that all the love potions brewed for her by the Witch of Fraddam were of no avail, she married the old lord – mainly, it is said, to be revenged on the son.

The witch had a niece who, though poor, possessed considerable beauty; she was called Bitha. This young girl was frequently employed by her aunt and the lady of Godolphin to aid them in

their spells on the young Pengerswick, and, as a natural conse-
quence, she fell desperately in love with him herself. Bitha ingrati-
ated herself with the lady of Pengerswick, now the stepmother of
the young man, and was selected as her maid. This gave her many
opportunities of seeing and speaking to young Pengerswick, and
her passion increased. The old stepdame was still passionately fond
of the young man, and never let a chance escape her which she
thought likely to lead to the excitement of passion in his heart
towards her. In all her attempts she failed. Her love was turned to
hate; and having seen her stepson in company with Bitha, this hate
was quickened by the more violent jealousy. Every means which
her wicked mind could devise were employed to destroy the young
man. Bitha had learned from her aunt, the Witch of Fraddam,
much of her art, and she devoted herself to counteract the spells of
her mistress.

The stepmother failing to accomplish her ends, resolved to ruin
young Pengerswick with his father. She persuaded the old man that
his son really entertained a violent passion for her, and that she was
compelled to confine herself to her tower in fear. The aged woman
prevailed on Lord Pengerswick to hire a gang of outlandish sailors
to carry his son away and sell him for a slave, giving him to believe
that she should herself in a short time present him with an heir.

The young Pengerswick escaped all their plots, and at his own
good time he disappeared from the castle, and for a long period
was never heard of.

The mistress and maid plotted and counter-plotted to secure the
old Pengerswick's wealth; and when he was on his death-bed, Bitha
informed him of the vile practices of his wife, and consoled him
with the information that he was dying from the effects of poison
given him by her.

The young lord, after long years, returned from some Eastern
lands with a princess for his wife, learned in all the magic sciences
of those enchanted lands. He found his stepmother shut up in her
chamber, with her skin covered with scales like a serpent, from the
effects of the poisons which she had so often been distilling for the

old lord and his son. She refused to be seen, and eventually cast herself into the sea, to the relief of all parties.

Bitha fared not much better. She lived on the Downs in St Hilary; and from the poisonous fumes she had inhaled, and from her dealings with the devil, her skin became the colour of that of a toad.

The pirate wrecker and the death ship

One lovely evening in the autumn, a strange ship was seen at a short distance from Cape Cornwall. The little wind there was blew from the land, but she did not avail herself of it. She was evidently permitted to drift with the tide, which was flowing southward and curving in round Whitesand Bay towards the Land's-End. The vessel, from her peculiar rig, created no small amount of alarm amongst the fishermen, since it told them that she was manned by pirates; and a large body of men and women watched her movements from behind the rocks at Caraglose. At length, when within a couple of pistol-shots off the shore, a boat was lowered and manned. Then a man, whose limited movements showed him to be heavily ironed, was brought to the side of the ship and evidently forced – for several pistols were held at his head – into the boat, which then rowed rapidly to the shore in Priest's Cove. The waves of the Atlantic Ocean fell so gently on the strand, that there was no difficulty in beaching the boat. The prisoner was made to stand up, and his ponderous chains were removed from his arms and ankles. In a frenzy of passion he attacked the sailors, but they were too many and too strong for him, and the fight terminated by his being thrown into the water, and left to scramble up on the dry sands. They pushed the boat off with a wild shout, and this man stood uttering fearful imprecations on his former comrades.

It subsequently became known that this man was so monstrously wicked that even the pirates would no longer endure him, and hence they had recourse to this means of ridding themselves of him.

It is not necessary to tell how this wretch settled himself at Tregaseal, and lived by a system of wrecking, pursued with unheard-of cruelties and cunning. 'It's too frightful to tell,' says my correspondent, 'what was said about his doings. We scarcely believed half of the vile things we heard, till we saw what took place at his death. But one can't say he died, because he was taken off bodily. We shall never know the scores, perhaps hundreds of ships that old sinner has brought on the cliffs, by fastening his lantern to the neck of his horse, with its head tied close to the fore-foot. The horse, when driven along the cliff, would, by its motion, cause the lantern to be taken for the stemlight of a ship; then the vessel would come right in on the rocks, since those on board would expect to find plenty of sea-room and, if any of the poor sailors escaped a watery grave, the old wretch would give them a worse death, by knocking them on the head with his hatchet, or cutting off their hands as they tried to grasp the ledges of the rocks.

A life of extreme wickedness was at length closed with circumstances of unusual terror – so terrible, that the story is told with feelings of awe even at the present day. The old wretch fought lustily with death, but at length the time of his departure came. It was in the time of the barley-harvest. Two men were in a field on the cliff, a little below the house, mowing. A universal calm prevailed, and there was not a breath of wind to stir the calm. Suddenly a breeze passed by them, and they heard the words 'The time is come, but the man isn't come.' These words appeared to float in the breeze from the sea, and consequently it attracted their attention. Looking out to sea, they saw a black, heavy, square-rigged ship, with all her sails set, coming in against wind and tide, and not a hand to be seen on board. The sky became black as night around the ship, and as she came under the cliff – and she came so close to the top of the masts could scarcely be perceived – the darkness resolved itself into a lurid storm-cloud, which extended high into the air. The sun shone brilliantly over the country, except on the house of the pirate at Tregaseal – that was wrapt in the deep shadow of the cloud.

The men, in terror, left their work; they found all the neighbours gathered around the door of the pirate's cottage, none of them daring to enter it. Parson had been sent for by the terrified peasants, this divine being celebrated for his power of driving away evil spirits.

The dying wrecker was in a state of agony, crying out, in tones of the most intense terror, 'The devil is tearing at me with nails like the claws of a hawk! Put out the sailors with their bloody hands!' and using, in the paroxysms of pain, the most profane imprecations. The parson, the doctor, and two of the bravest of the fishermen were the only persons in the room. They related that at one moment the room was as dark as the grave, and that at the next it was so light that every hair on the old man's head could be seen standing on end. The parson used all his influence to dispel the evil spirit. His powers were so potent that he reduced the devil to the size of a fly, but he could not put him out of the room. All this time the room appeared as if filled with the sea, with the waves surging violently to and fro, and one could hear the breakers roaring, as if standing on the edge of the cliff in a storm. At last there was a fearful crash of thunder, and a blaze of the intensest lightning. The house appeared on fire, and the ground shook, as if with an earthquake. All rushed in terror from the house, leaving the dying man to his fate.

The storm raged with fearful violence, but appeared to contract its dimensions. The black cloud, which was first seen to come in with the black ship, was moving, with a violent internal motion, over the wrecker's house. The cloud rolled together, smaller and smaller, and suddenly, with the blast of a whirlwind, it passed from Tregaseal to the ship, and she was impelled, amidst the flashes of lightning and roarings of thunder, away over the sea.

The dead body of the pirate-wrecker lay a ghastly spectacle, with eyes expanded and the mouth partly open, still retaining the aspect of his last mortal terror. As everyone hated him, they all desired to remove his corpse as rapidly as possible from the sight of man. A rude coffin was rapidly prepared, and the body was carefully cased in its boards. They tell me the coffin was carried to the churchyard, but that it was too light to have contained the body, and that it was followed by a black pig, which joined the company forming the procession, nobody knew where, and disappeared nobody knew when. When they reached the church stile, a storm, similar in its character to that which heralded the wrecker's death, came on. The bearers of the coffin were obliged to leave it without the churchyard stile, and rush into the church for safety. The storm lasted long and raged with violence, and all was as dark as night. A sudden blaze of light, more vivid than before, was seen, and those who had the hardihood to look out saw that the lightning had set fire to the coffin, and it was being borne away through the air, blazing and whirling wildly in the grasp of such a whirlwind as no man ever witnessed before or since.

The witch of Treva

Once on a time, long ago, there lived at Treva, a hamlet in Zennor, a wonderful old lady deeply skilled in necromancy. Her charms, spells, and dark incantations made her the terror of the neighbourhood. However, this old lady failed to impress her husband with any belief in her supernatural powers nor did he fail to proclaim his unbelief aloud.

One day this sceptic came home to dinner, and found, being exceedingly hungry, to his bitter disappointment, that not only was there no dinner to eat, but that there was no meat in the house. His rage was great, but all he could get from his wife was, 'I couldn't get meat out of the stones, could I ?' It was in vain to give the reins to passion, the old woman told him, and he must know 'that hard words buttered no parsnips.'

Well, at length he resolved to put his wife's powers to the proof, and he quietly but determinedly told her that he would be the death of her if she did not get him some dinner; but if in half an hour she gave him some good cooked meat, he would believe all she had boasted of her power, and be submissive to her for ever. St Ives, the nearest market-town, was five miles off; but nothing doubting, the witch put on her bonnet and cloak, and started. Her husband watched her from their cottage door, down the hill; and at the bottom of the hill, he saw his wife quietly place herself on the ground and disappear. In her place a fine hare ran on at its full speed.

He was not a little startled, but he waited, and within the half-hour in walked his wife with 'good flesh and taties all ready for ait-ing'. There was no longer any doubt, and the poor husband lived in fear of the witch of Treva to the day of her death. This event took place after a few years, and it is said the room was full of evil spirits, and that the old woman's shrieks were awful to hear. Howbeit, peace in the shape of pale-faced death came to her at last, and then a black cloud rested over the house when all the heavens were clear and blue.

She was borne to the grave by six aged men, carried, as is the custom, underhand. When they were about half way between the house and the church, a hare started from the roadside and leaped over the coffin. The terrified bearers let the corpse fall to the ground, and ran away. Another lot of men took up the coffin and proceeded. They had not gone far when puss was suddenly seen seated on the coffin, and again the coffin was abandoned. After long consultation, and being persuaded by the parson to carry the old woman very quickly into the churchyard, while he walked before, six others made the attempt, and as the parson never ceased to repeat the Lord's Prayer, all went on quietly. Arrived at the church stile, they rested the corpse, the parson paused to commence the ordinary burial service, and there stood the hare, which, as soon as the clergyman began 'I am the resurrection and the life,' uttered a diabolical howl, changed into a black, unshapen creature, and disappeared.

Dorcas, the spirit of Polbreen Mine

Polbreen Mine is situated at the foot of the hill known as St Agnes Beacon. In one of the small cottages which immediately adjoins the mine once lived a woman called Dorcas. Beyond this we know little of her life; but we are concerned chiefly with her death, which, we are told, was suicidal.

From some cause, which is not related, Dorcas grew weary of life, and one unholy night she left her house and flung herself into one of the deep shafts of Polbreen Mine, at the bottom of which her dead and broken body was discovered. The remnant of humanity was brought to the surface; and after the laws of the time with regard to suicides had been fulfilled, the body of Dorcas was buried.

Her presence, however, still remained in the mine. She appears ordinarily to take a malicious delight in tormenting the industrious miner, calling him by name, and alluring him from his tasks. This was carried on by her to such an extent, that when a 'tributer' had made a poor month, he was asked if he had 'been chasing Dorcas?'

Dorcas was usually only a voice. It has been said by some that they have seen her in the mine, but this is doubted by the miners generally, who refer the spectral appearance to the fears of their comrade.

But it is stated as an incontrovertible fact, that more than one man who has met the spirit in the levels of the mine has had his clothes torn off his back; whether in anger or in sport, is not clearly made out. On one occasion, and on one occasion only, Dorcas appears to have acted kindly. Two miners, who for distinction's sake we will call Martin and Jacky, were at work in their end, and at the time busily at work 'beating the borer'.

The name of Jacky was distinctly uttered between the blows. He stopped and listened – all was still. They proceeded with their task: a blow on the iron rod. – 'Jacky.' Another blow. – 'Jacky.' They pause – all is silent. 'Well, thee wert called, Jacky,' said Martin, 'go and see.'

Jacky was, however, either afraid, or he thought himself the fool of his senses.

Work was resumed, and 'Jacky ! Jacky ! Jacky !' was called more vehemently and distinctly than before.

Jacky threw down his heavy hammer, and went from his companion, resolved to satisfy himself as to the caller.

He had not proceeded many yards from the spot on which he had been standing at work, when a mass of rock fell from the roof of the level, weighing many tons, which would have crushed him to death. Martin had been stooping, holding the borer, and a projecting corner of rock just above him turned off the falling mass. He was securely enclosed, and they had to dig him out, but he escaped without injury. Jacky declared to his dying day that he owed his life to Dorcas.

Although Dorcas's shaft remains a part of Polbreen Mine, I am informed by the agent that her presence has departed.

The voice from the sea

A fisherman or a pilot was walking one night on the sands at Porth-Towan, when all was still save the monotonous fall of the light waves upon the sand. He distinctly heard a voice from the sea exclaiming,— 'The hour is come, but not the man.' This was repeated three times, when a black figure, like that of a man, appeared on the top of the hill. It paused for a moment, then rushed impetuously down the steep incline, over the sands, and was lost in the sea. In different forms this story is told all around the Cornish coast.

Pengerswick Castle

This castellated building – for it does not now admit of being called a castle, notwithstanding its embattled turrets and its machicolated gate – is situated in a hollow running down to Pengerswick Cove, in the Mount's Bay, where there never could have been anything to defend; and certainly there is nothing to induce any one to incur the cost of such a building.

Mr Milliton, in the reign of Henry VIII, slew in the streets of London a man in a drunken brawl. He fled, and went to sea. It is not known to what part of the world he went, but we are told that he became excessively rich; so rich, indeed, that 'when he loaded his ass with his gold, the weight was so great as to break the poor animal's back.' Returning to his country, and not daring to appear in any of the large towns, he bought the manor of Pengerswick, and built this castle, to defend himself, in the event of his being approached by any of the officers of the law.

A miserable man, Milliton is said to have lived in a secret chamber in this tower, and to have been visited only by his most trusted friends. Deeply deploring the crime that had condemned him to seclusion from the world, he spent his dreary hours in ornamenting his dwelling. His own story is supposed to be told in the painting of an overladen ass in one room, with a black-letter legend, importing that a miser is like an ass loaded with riches, who, without attending to his golden burden, feeds on thistles. There is also a carving of water wearing a hollow in a stone, and under it the word 'Perseverance'. Of the death of Milliton we have no account.

There is very little doubt but that Pengerswick Castle is very much older than the time of Milliton; indeed tradition informs us that he purchased the place. The legends previously given, and others in my possession, refer to a much earlier period. The castle was, it is said, surrounded by trees; but John Hals, who inherited the property, had all the timber cut down and sold.